Understanding

ALCOHOL
& DRINKING PROBLEMS

Dr Jonathan Chick

Published by Family Doctor Publications Limited
in association with the British Medical Association

IMPORTANT NOTICE

This book is intended not as a substitute for personal medical advice but as a supplement to that advice for the patient who wishes to understand more about his/her condition.

Before taking any form of treatment YOU SHOULD ALWAYS CONSULT YOUR MEDICAL PRACTITIONER.

In particular (without limit) you should note that advances in medical science occur rapidly and some of the information about drugs and treatment contained in this booklet may very soon be out of date.

THIS IS THE 1999 EDITION

All rights reserved. No part of this publication may be reproduced, or stored in a retrieval system, or transmitted, in any form or by any means, electronic, mechanical, photocopying, recording and/or otherwise, without the prior written permission of the publishers. The right of Dr Jonathan Chick to be identified as the author of this work has been asserted in accordance with the Copyright, Designs and Patents Act 1988 Sections 77 and 78.

© Family Doctor Publications 1997, 1999
Reprinted 1999

Family Doctor Publications, 10 Butchers Row, Banbury, Oxon OX16 8JH

Medical Editor: Dr Tony Smith
Consultant Editors: Mary Fox and Lynne Low
Cover Artist: Dave Eastbury
Cartoonist: Dave Eastbury
Design: Neil Deacon, London and MPG Design, Blandford Forum, Dorset
Printing: Reflex Litho, Thetford, Norfolk, using acid-free paper

ISBN: 1 898205 23 X

Contents

Introduction

Mr Roberts was finding work increasingly difficult and dreaded the tension he felt in the mornings. He had enjoyed a drink after work for years, but now his wife and children were complaining about his irritability and asking why he was no longer the reliable husband and father they knew. When his doctor checked his blood pressure he also asked him about his drinking. An explanation of how alcohol could actually cause tension did not make sense to him at first, but he agreed to have three weeks free of alcohol – and he felt much better. He decided to cut drinking out of his life. With his family's support and advice from his GP, he found this much easier than he had feared, and was soon back to his former vigour and enthusiasm for family life and work.

Out of the UK population of 56 million people, 36 million of us are regular drinkers. 2 million are heavy drinkers, and there are a million men and women in Britain who have, or have had, a serious drinking problem. Of those, 200,000 are dependent on alcohol each day of

their lives. More women are now drinking than ever before in this century. While alcohol-related problems used to affect far more men than women, women now seek counselling for drinking problems as frequently as men.

This book explains how alcohol can have a variety of harmful as well as pleasant effects. It gives guidance on how to change a drinking pattern and succeed – whether by cutting down or abstaining completely.

KEY POINTS

✓ 36 million people in the UK are regular drinkers

✓ Women seek counselling for drinking problems as frequently as men

What determines our drinking habits?

WHAT IS ALCOHOL?

Beer, wine, spirits, cider – and the scores of other drinks fermented or distilled around the world – all contain ethanol. Ethanol, which belongs to a group of chemical substances called alcohols, is produced when yeast assists the fermentation of sugar to form ethanol and carbon dioxide. The amount of ethanol produced is controlled by the quantity of sugar added, or until the ethanol level reaches 14 per cent by volume, after which the yeast cannot survive. The carbon dioxide produced forms the 'head' on a glass of beer, and the bubbles in champagne.

The process of distillation – boiling off and concentrating the ethanol part of the beverage – was discovered in the Middle East in AD 800 by a man called Jahir ibn Hayyan. Distillation allows more concentrated and potent alcoholic drinks to be produced.

Other constituents (sometimes called congeners) contribute to the taste we may enjoy, but can also cause headache and hangover if we have drunk a lot. The amount of congener varies – drinks with a dark colour such as red wine or brandy contain more congeners, and so cause more hangover than pale drinks.

Although other constituents give drinks their colour, taste and character, it is ethanol that causes a change in our brain. This change can, if the circumstances are right, lead us to feel merry and talkative, or relaxed and sleepy. It is ethanol that helps us let our hair down. Celebrating, marking special events and meeting up with friends have become occasions for drinking. The advertising and marketing of the drinks industry are designed to make sure that we continue to believe in the good things about alcohol.

Ethanol also causes some of the unpleasant effects of being intoxicated – such as slowing our thinking and our reactions,

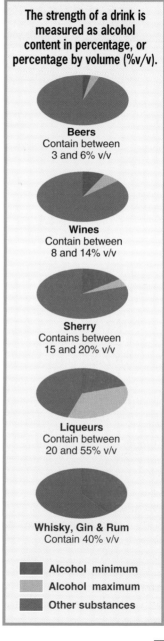

The strength of a drink is measured as alcohol content in percentage, or percentage by volume (%v/v).

Beers
Contain between 3 and 6% v/v

Wines
Contain between 8 and 14% v/v

Sherry
Contains between 15 and 20% v/v

Liqueurs
Contain between 20 and 55% v/v

Whisky, Gin & Rum
Contain 40% v/v

Alcohol minimum
Alcohol maximum
Other substances

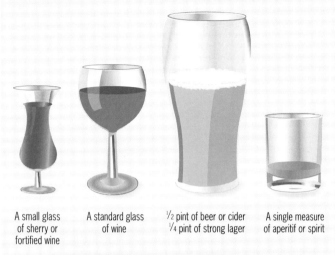

A small glass of sherry or fortified wine

A standard glass of wine

$1/2$ pint of beer or cider
$1/4$ pint of strong lager

A single measure of aperitif or spirit

A bottle of spirits – brandy, whisky or gin – contains about 30 units

irritability and the tendency to do things on the spur of the moment which may be regretted later.

WHAT ARE COMMON MEASUREMENTS OF ALCOHOL?

Many people nowadays talk in terms of 'units' of alcohol, to measure amount. Most British pub measures of spirits – $1/6$ or $1/5$ gill – is about one unit, and contains the same amount of alcohol as the items in the box.

The strength of a drink is measured as alcohol content in percentage, or percentage by volume (%v/v).

For purposes of measuring alcohol concentration in blood, we use the amount of alcohol (in milligrams) found in 100 millilitres of blood. This is written as 'mg per 100 ml blood' or 'mg%'.

As a very rough guide, one unit of alcohol drunk on an empty stomach results in a peak alcohol level of 15 mg% in a man. This figure will be up to 30 per cent higher in a woman, for reasons we explain below. The present legal limit for driving is set at 80 mg%. At this level, the risk of having a road accident is more than doubled. In experiments, bus drivers with alcohol levels of only 50 mg% (below the legal limit) thought that they could drive through obstacles too narrow for their buses. Concentrations of 400 mg% could block the brain's breathing control centre and be fatal, especially if sedative drugs have been taken as well.

In breath tests, the units used are micrograms (μg) per 100 ml of breath. The breathalyser measures the alcohol contained in each 100 ml of breath. The present legal limit for driving is 35 mg per 100 ml breath.

On average, the body removes alcohol at about 15 mg% or one unit per hour. This means that a person who drinks eight pints one night may still be over the legal limit to drive to work the next day.

ARE WE DRINKING MORE THAN WE USED TO?

Compared with 100 years ago, the British are probably drinking less. Gin and beer used to be cheap, and we were great importers of brandy and wine. In 1914 Lloyd George, the British Prime Minister, was worried about the effect of alcohol on the industrial effort needed for the war, so restrictions were increased on the sale of drink. Consumption fell dramatically and remained low in the depression years between the wars. It began to increase in 1950, as prosperity in Britain returned.

Tax on alcoholic drinks had limited drinking, but less so from 1950 to 1980 as the tax imposed was a smaller proportion of

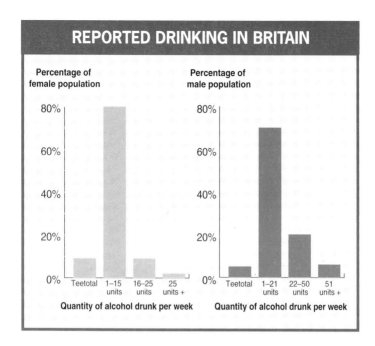

REPORTED DRINKING IN BRITAIN

Percentage of female population

Quantity of alcohol drunk per week

Teetotal | 1–15 units | 16–25 units | 25 units +

Percentage of male population

Quantity of alcohol drunk per week

Teetotal | 1–21 units | 22–50 units | 51 units +

people's wages. In real terms, alcohol became cheaper. From 1965 to 1987, the amount each adult was drinking, on average, doubled. Spirits made up less of the total and wine became more popular. The steepest rise was among women.

Today, although the average amount consumed per person has levelled off, the number of deaths from alcoholic liver disease is still climbing.

Our European neighbours, except for the Scandinavians, drink more per person than we do in Britain. The French and Italians have now reduced their total consumption a great deal as drinking wine each day at meals is going out of fashion. So their wine producers are glad to be selling more to the British!

WHAT AFFECTS INDIVIDUAL DRINKING HABITS?
Genetics

Some people dislike the effects or taste of alcohol – they can either avoid it or train themselves to drink. Others like the effect from the start. Drinking problems run in families. This is partly because a child who grows up with one or both parents drinking heavily may learn to do the same. However, there is also a genetic factor. Children who are fostered or adopted at birth have a drinking problem more often than other adopted or fostered children if one of their real parents had a drinking problem.

Identical twins, who share an identical chemical blueprint, tend to drink in a similar way because differences between people's liking for alcohol are partly due to differences in body and brain chemistry. In pairs of twins where one has a drinking problem, the other twin is more likely to have a drinking problem if they are an identical pair (exactly the same genes) rather than a non-identical pair (whose genes are only as alike as those of other brothers and sisters). There is probably a genetic factor involved in whether people enjoy the effects of alcohol or not, and also in whether or not alcohol causes problems or addictions.

Social factors

Our pattern of drinking tends to be similar to that of our friends. For many people their circle of friends develops in their teenage years and changes little. People like to drink for the sociability and humour that goes with it, and because it helps them break their routine. Second to watching TV, going for a drink is Britain's favourite leisure activity.

A new job or getting married can alter an established pattern. Spouses can have an influence on their partners' drinking. For instance, when two sisters who are identical twins stay unmarried, they are likely to go through adult life drinking in a similar pattern, whereas if one or both marry, their drinking patterns may begin to differ.

In their later years, many people drink less than they did when they were 18 to 25.

CASE HISTORY: JANET

Moira and Janet are identical twins and even lived together when they both got office jobs in the centre of London. Janet's manager was an extrovert golfer who loved the club life. At first

MOIRA AND JANET WERE TWINS, BOTH WORKING IN LONDON...

COME ON MOIRA WE'LL BE LATE FOR WORK...

JANET MARRIED HER MANAGER...

I WISH HE WOULD SPEND LESS TIME DRINKING, MOIRA!

she was resentful when his bachelor lifestyle continued after they were married, but she joined in with him rather than try to change him. Janet had not liked alcohol as a teenager and Moira became distressed as her sister gradually extended her pattern of drinking to become someone who, it seemed to Moira, always had a drink in her hand.

HAVE ANOTHER ONE, JAN!

WHAT'S UP WITH JANET SHE'S CHANGED SO MUCH!

Work patterns

A person's job influences his or her drinking. Jobs with high exposure to alcohol include the building industry, the drinks trade, hotels and restaurants, and work which takes people away from home – such as the armed services and sales travelling.

Religious beliefs

Some faiths recommend strict moderation or even total abstinence and the faithful adhere to this. There are religious writings going back thousands of years about the problems alcohol can cause. Some religions give a specific place to alcohol, such as wine in Jewish family ceremonies. Occasionally members of strict communities such as Moslem societies may drink but risk disapproval. They may run into difficulties controlling their intake because they have not learned moderate drinking in their family.

Those who practise a religion are able to meet friends and take part in social gatherings without alcohol. This is in contrast to most social occasions and even some sporting events in our society, which usually involve drinking.

Drinking 'to cope'

Alcohol is our favourite drug. Occasionally people drink more because they feel it helps them cope with a problem or blots it out. However, one problem can become two, as the individual gets into the vicious circle called dependence, and the drinking escalates (see page 47). Dependence on alcohol can be a major problem, because drinkers begin to be unable to control how much or how often they drink, and find it very difficult to change. We explain this later.

KEY POINTS

✓ How much we drink depends partly on the genes that we inherit from our parents

✓ Some occupations lead to heavy drinking

✓ Drinking to solve a problem can lead to two problems

Alcohol and health

How the body handles alcohol

Alcohol is absorbed from the stomach and small intestine into the blood stream. The rate at which it is absorbed varies – it is most rapid on an empty stomach, so that a high peak level is quickly reached, and the person feels drunk quickly. Food in the stomach slows down its absorption by up to 50 per cent, thus reducing peak blood alcohol level. This also means that the same amount of alcohol stays longer in the body when the stomach is full than if it is empty.

The alcohol from wine and sherry reaches the blood stream more quickly than from beer, because it is more concentrated. Sugar in sweet drinks retards absorption, whereas the bubbles of carbon dioxide in champagne or gin and tonic accelerate it.

Alcohol is distributed throughout the body so that most tissues – the heart, the brain and the muscles – get the same concentration as present in the blood. The liver receives a higher concentration. Little alcohol enters fat, which has a poor blood supply. Women have more of their body weight as fat and less as muscles and blood. This explains why a woman of the same weight as a man and who has drunk the same amount of alcohol will have a higher level of alcohol in blood and tissue. Women also break down less alcohol in the stomach than men. Women are therefore generally able to tolerate less alcohol than men. In pregnant women alcohol crosses the placenta into the fetus.

Alcohol is metabolised by the liver first to a substance called acetaldehyde which is very toxic. It is thought that acetaldehyde may be responsible for some of the physical damage caused by alcohol. Acetaldehyde is quickly changed to a non-toxic substance called acetate. The chemical processes in the liver are complex and require many enzymes, which are substances that assist the chemical processes. The way the liver deals with alcohol can be accelerated or retarded by medications which affect the enzymes. It also varies according to the amount of alcohol drunk, the amount that is normally drunk (what the enzymes are used to dealing with) and whether the liver is healthy or not. Too much alcohol is toxic to the liver, and the process of handling alcohol can be slowed when the liver is diseased, as in cirrhosis of the liver, which occurs after long-term alcohol abuse (see Harm from heavy drinking on page 19).

Only two to five per cent of alcohol gets excreted without processing, either in the urine or in the breath. Although breath concentrations are low, they reflect accurately the blood alcohol level, and this forms the basis of the breathalyser test.

Why can some people 'hold their drink' better?

The amount of alcohol people can tolerate depends on a variety of factors including whether food is taken as well. As explained earlier, women may get a higher level in the blood than a man, after drinking the same amount. The bigger a person is, the more he or she can drink without appearing intoxicated. The liver enzymes of a person with a regular drinking habit also become more efficient at handling alcohol, and so people who are used to alcohol can burn it off slightly quicker than first-time drinkers. Children are therefore very susceptible, being smaller in size than adults, and less experienced drinkers. It is mainly the adjustments that the brain cells make that

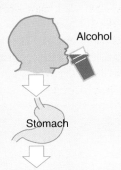

Alcohol

Stomach

Absorbed into <u>blood stream</u> in stomach
and small intestines

Goes around body in blood stream
and enters organs with rich blood
supply including:

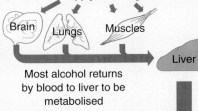

Brain   Lungs   Muscles

Most alcohol returns
by blood to liver to be
metabolised

Liver

In liver, alcohol is
broken down by
chemical reaction.
Waste from this
process goes in the
blood to the kidneys
to be excreted in
the urine

Blood

Kidneys

Only 2 – 5%
bypasses liver and is
excreted without
metabolism

Excreted in
the urine

IMMEDIATE EFFECTS OF ALCOHOL ON THE BODY

- Increases the heart rate
- Dilates the skin blood vessels
- Stimulates the release of gastric juices
- High doses irritate the stomach lining
- May have a diuretic effect – more urine is produced
- Speech may become slurred
- Memory is impaired
- Eyes focus with difficulty
- Movement and coordination may be impaired
- Effects emotional control and judgement
- High doses cause unconciousness which puts people at grave risk of choking
- High doses may block the breathing centre in the brain

allow regular drinkers to drink without initially showing much effect. This tolerance of the brain cells may be the beginnings of dependence on alcohol for some drinkers.

What are the effects of alcohol on the body?

Alcohol causes a small increase in heart rate, and dilates the skin blood vessels, producing the characteristic flush. The flush is severe in some people of Chinese or Japanese origin. This causes a feeling of warmth, although body temperature may actually fall because heat from the body is lost through the skin. Drinking brandy from the neck cask of a St Bernard dog who has rescued you in snow could lead to hypothermia! Alcohol stimulates the release of gastric juices and acids, and can lead to inflammation of the stomach lining. Some alcoholic drinks also have a diuretic effect, causing more urine to be produced.

However, most people drink for the effects of alcohol on the brain. At blood levels of about 50 mg% most people feel relaxed and carefree. At higher concentrations more brain functions are affected. Speech becomes slurred, memory is impaired and the eyes focus with difficulty. At 100 mg% movement starts to become careless and clumsy, and emotional control and judgement may be impaired. Alcohol can cause people to take more risks. At 200–300 mg% most people are very drunk, and may become unconscious. The level at which alcohol becomes fatal varies – what a hard drinking man regularly tolerates may kill a young girl who has never had a drink before. After the level of alcohol in the blood has peaked, there is a phase when the individual may feel tired, depressed and perhaps irritable.

What causes a hangover?

The effects of the congeners in drinks cause the nausea, headache, tremulousness and tiredness that we recognise as a hangover. Dehydration may contribute, and drinking alcohol with sufficient water may prevent some symptoms. However, as blood levels of alcohol fall during the night, there is a rebound wakefulness, and some of the heightened sensitivity and restlessness is caused by withdrawal. Contrary to popular myth, mixing drinks does not cause a hangover, and neither does avoiding mixing prevent one! It is more likely that if you do mix drinks, you are taking a large dose of alcohol, which gives you more of a headache the next day.

Harm from heavy drinking: the immediate problems

Health risk

The greatest problem is that a large enough dose of alcohol can kill by blocking the breathing centre in the brain. Even if the amount taken is not directly fatal, the deep unconsciousness it causes puts people at risk of dying from exposure, or choking and suffocating on their own vomit. Other short-term problems include dehydration and low blood sugar, which can be dangerous for young, elderly and diabetic people.

Accidents

The most common reason for drinkers seeing a doctor is an injury caused by drunkenness. When people are drunk they are a danger to themselves and to others. Alcohol is associated with the accidents shown in the box.

HARM FROM ALCOHOL

Alcohol consumption is implicated in:

- 80% of deaths from fires
- 65% of serious head injuries
- 50% of murders
- 40% of road traffic accidents
- 30% of accidents in the home

Alcohol is also a factor in rail, shipping and airplane accidents. One-third of private pilots killed are believed to have alcohol in their blood. The accident rate for heavy drinkers at work is three times the normal. About 60 per cent of fatal accidents at work are alcohol related. For more information on drinking and driving, see page 67.

Alcohol also leads to greater risk-taking, and may lead to a person making him or herself vul-

nerable to crime and assault, both physical and sexual.

HARM FROM HEAVY DRINKING: LONGER-TERM PROBLEMS

Heavy drinking means more than 5 units per day for women or 7 units per day for men. Safe limits are up to a maximum of 3 units per day for women and 4 units per day for

men. Even so, [...] Officer has [...] drinking one to [...] fers the best h [...] risk, and that [...] to a maximum [...] problems. And the more the safe limit is exceeded, the more likely illness becomes.

Heart and circulation

Although drinking one to three units a day may help prevent heart attacks and angina, there is another type of heart disease which people drinking over 10 units per day can develop. It results from damage to the heart muscle and causes breathlessness and palpitations (a fluttering feeling in the heart), swelling of the ankles and accumulation of fluid in the lungs.

Alcohol can cause strokes, partly as a result of high blood pressure, so those people with high blood pressure should cut down their drinking.

Digestive system

The irritation to your stomach lining caused by alcohol can cause loss of appetite. When severe, it results in pain, vomiting and bleeding.

The pancreas lies behind your stomach and is also sensitive to alcohol. When its cells become inflamed the pain is very severe. If it becomes damaged permanently, your pancreas cannot make enough

A UNIT OF ALCOHOL IS

A small glass of sherry or fortified wine

½ pint of beer or cider ¼ pint of strong lager

A single measure of aperitif or spirit

A standard glass of wine

A bottle of spirits – brandy, whisky, or gin – contains about 30 units

...d diabetes follows. ... that break alcohol down ... produced properly and diarrhea can result.

Liver

Liver problems can be deceptive. Although a blood test from your family doctor could show that alcohol is causing harm to your liver, you may notice nothing for years. By then it can be too late.

Alcohol can cause several problems with the liver. In mild cases, fat gets deposited in the liver, causing the cells to bulge. The liver increases in size, giving rise to vague abdominal discomfort and nausea.

In more serious cases, alcoholic hepatitis occurs. Here, the liver cells are inflamed, and damaged. The person may feel well, but more often feels ill and weak, and may be jaundiced. Jaundice is a yellowing of the skin caused by the accumulation, in the blood, of a substance called bilirubin which is then deposited in the skin. One of the liver's roles is to process bilirubin to

keep the level steady, but when it is diseased, this process breaks down, and the level of bilirubin starts to climb.

In the final stage of alcohol damage, cirrhosis occurs. Here, the alcohol has caused serious and permanent damage. The cells of the liver are destroyed, and massive scarring takes place, so that the liver itself becomes distorted.

The liver's ability to function properly is greatly compromised, and it may be unable to deal adequately with metabolising drugs and alcohol. A person with cirrhosis is deeply jaundiced, has an enlarged liver and spleen, and swelling of the abdomen and legs with water (oedema).

The scarring and distortion block the flow of blood into the liver. The back pressure this causes leads to varicose veins swelling up in the stomach and gullet – and these can bleed and bleed.

The only effective cure for life-threatening cirrhosis is liver transplantation. Because of the shortage of donor organs, doctors may be unwilling to recommend someone who has abused alcohol for this treatment, unless a firm undertaking to stop drinking is agreed. If cirrhosis has not reached the life-threatening stage, stopping drinking will often halt further damage and allow a reasonable quality of life.

Cancer

Alcohol can cause cancer. Drinkers are more prone than others to cancer in the mouth, throat and gullet. Smoking contributes to these too. Large studies of women in the United States of America have shown that breast cancer is linked to heavier drinking.

Brain and nerves

Some heavy drinkers lose mental faculties, especially the ability to remember new things and recent events. It is an exaggeration of what happens in old age. Others damage their balance mechanism. Others get pins and needles in the feet and hands and, combined with alcohol-induced loss of muscle, this leads to great difficulty in walking.

People who drink sometimes do not take a balanced diet and this can result in vitamin deficiency. Alcohol reduces the body's ability to absorb vitamins from food and a deficiency of vitamin B_1 (thiamine) is linked to nerve and brain damage in heavy drinkers.

Blood

Alcohol causes changes in the blood cells. Your doctor may unexpectedly find an abnormal test result, due to alcohol, when your blood is taken for some other reason. Regular drinkers may have enlarged red blood cells, but this itself is not dangerous. Blood tests to check how the liver is functioning may show an abnormal result long before liver disease develops. Your doctor will explain whether a result indicates serious illness. Gamma-glutamyl transferase (GGT) measurement is the liver test that is most sensitive to drinking.

If you are planning to reduce your alcohol intake, you can ask your doctor to repeat the tests. This gives you and your doctor a way of measuring whether you are being successful in cutting down! There is now a new blood test called carbohydrate-deficient transferase (CDT) which is more accurate than older tests in showing excessive drinking and changes in drinking.

Mental illness

Alcohol can cause mental illness. It alters the brain chemistry to cause depressed mood. This can, of course, also harm important relationships with friends and family.

Jealous delusions can develop. It may be believed, wrongly, that a partner is having an affair and drinking can cause the situation to be blown up out of all proportion.

Fortunately quite rare, there is another illness in which the brain can be so damaged that hallucinations occur which may go on for weeks or months. The 'voices' may say threatening or derogatory things which are frightening. This can nearly always be cured by med-

ical treatment and by staying away from all alcohol.

Your complexion

Regular heavy drinkers give their habit away by their red and blotchy face, with tiny extra blood vessels in the cheeks and eyes. The bulging red nose only comes after 15 years of tippling!

Some people have a condition called psoriasis in which the skin develops red patches and the surface layer is white and flaky. It comes and goes – and heavy drinking can bring on an episode.

Your weight

Alcoholic drinks are calories without vitamins. When alcohol is broken down by the liver, it forms fat and sugar, which are both high in calories. A glass of wine or half a pint of lager contains about the same number of calories as a thick slice of bread and butter. Therefore drinkers can put on weight. The beer belly is well named – three pints of beer a day or 21 pints per week will increase your weight by about four pounds in four weeks. Two or three single gin and tonics a day will do the same. And, of course, the same will happen in the next four weeks – and so on!

Drinking a glass of sherry can stimulate your appetite, but drinking five or six units regularly without food irritates your stomach lining and causes nausea. This is why some drinkers lose weight and feel weak and easily tired.

BENEFITS TO HEALTH

The news on alcohol is not all bad. Used in moderation, some people

may have positive health benefits. An American study in an old people's home in 1960 found that by introducing a 'cocktail hour' in the ward each afternoon, incontinence fell from 76 to 27 per cent, and mobility improved from 21 per cent of patients to 75 per cent. Three-quarters of patients used to require sleeping tablets, but with the 'cocktail hour' nobody needed any. Small amounts of alcohol, taken in a controlled fashion, can make life seem a little more colourful, but should never be a solution to our problems.

Heart disease

Medical research has found that people who drink moderately – one to three units a day – have less chance than abstainers of getting heart disease. This probably only applies in middle age, and when there is a tendency to the high-risk fat/cholesterol pattern in the blood. As heart disease is a common cause of death in Western society, it means that their life expectancy is a little longer than either abstainers or heavy drinkers. We can, of course, reduce the chance that we will get heart disease in other ways – stopping smoking, losing weight, eating less animal fats and more fruit and vegetables, and taking more exercise.

Getting a job where we feel in control and achieve satisfaction helps too. People whose pattern is to drink one to three units per day tend to be in that category and often also have a sensible diet – this may explain their better health. Governments do not advise people to drink to protect their health – if we were told one or two drinks were good for us, we may imagine three or four would be even better!

Bones

In middle age and later, women who drink a little have stronger bones than those who are teetotal. Heavy drinking, though, can make bones thinner and may lead to more fractures. The advice, as always, must be moderation.

Sex

Does alcohol improve sex? For some people, a drink can increase their desire. If tension is reducing their enjoyment of sex then relaxing with alcohol can help. In men, large doses of alcohol block the nerves necessary for erection – thus raising fears about impotence.

If this happens more than once or twice he may get seriously worried about his sexual ability – and worrying about performance is a sure way to impair erections, until confidence is re-established with a sympathetic partner.

IS THERE A SAFE LIMIT?

For a woman, the chance of having liver disease or breast cancer begins to go up once she is drinking three units per day. Some people have more resistant bodies than others but we have no way yet of telling in advance who they are. A man's liver can stand slightly more, but five units per day (35 per week) has been shown to be the start of problems for some men. The safe limit is two units per day for women, three units per day for men.

SPECIAL CIRCUMSTANCES
Pregnancy

Animal tests have revealed that heavy drinking can alter genetic material, leading to abnormal development in the fetus. Most pregnancies with abnormal fetuses

DANGEROUS DRUGS WHEN TAKEN WITH ALCOHOL

- Benzodiazepines, e.g. diazepam (Valium)
- Barbiturates, e.g. phenobarbitone
- Some antidepressants, e.g. imipramine (Tofranil), dothiepin (Prothiaden), amitriptyline (Tryptizol)
- The antibiotic metronidazole (Flagyl)
- Some antihypertensive medication, e.g. isocarboxazid (Marplan), phenelzine (Nardil)
- Oral diabetic tablets
- Antiepileptic drugs, e.g. phenytoin (Epanutin)
- Warfarin
- Other tranquillisers

miscarry – and pregnant women who drink heavily have twice the rate of miscarriage compared with non-drinkers. If a woman drinks more than 10 units a day during pregnancy, she runs the risk of having a baby with 'fetal alcohol syndrome', in which the baby is mentally handicapped with abnormal facial features, and a variety of neurological, heart, bone and kidney defects.

Most authorities advise pregnant women to abstain from alcohol, or at the very least to restrict alcohol intake to the occasional drink, especially early in pregnancy.

Alcohol appears in breast milk in breast-feeding mothers, but the occasional drink before breast-feeding will do no harm.

Alcohol and prescribed drugs
The effect of alcohol on prescribed drugs depends on the drug, and also on whether alcohol is taken in a one-off binge, or as part of a chronic problem.

In the first instance, alcohol competes with the drug for liver enzymes, and so the drug is broken down more slowly and becomes 'stronger', and works for longer. This can be dangerous, as it is effectively an overdose.

The drugs in this category include those in the box.

The most common danger of taking alcohol while on a medication comes with any drug that has a sedative effect, however slight. The sedative effect of the alcoholic drink may double the sedative effect of the drug, resulting in accidents. Sedatives include tranquillisers, many antidepressants, antihistamines and sleeping tablets.

hen drinking is heavy and pro-
.ged, the effect is to speed up the
liver enzymes (as they get used to
dealing with a big load), and so
some drugs get dealt with quickly
as well, and thus have a lesser effect
than normal. Drug dosage may
need to be increased by the doctor.
The drugs in this category include
those in the box (right).

DRUGS AFFECTED BY ALCOHOL

- Drugs for epilepsy
- Some antibiotics
- Some drugs to lower blood pressure
- Some antidepressants

KEY POINTS

✓ Drinking on an empty stomach means that alcohol reaches the brain in a burst

✓ Drinking one to three units per day can reduce the chance of heart disease; more than that can harm health

✓ One unit has the same calories as a slice of bread and butter

✓ Alcohol is a factor in some types of cancer

Effects of drinking on daily life

DRINKING IN THE FAMILY

Having a drink on a special occasion is part of our culture. If families do this together and include teenagers, without people getting drunk, it helps the younger members learn to handle alcohol safely. A complete ban on alcohol can lead a teenager to rebel by drinking, to be different from the family – with all the risks that such behaviour involves.

When someone in the family drinks too much

Drinking can lead to changes in the way we react to people, which can damage relationships very badly.

A father becomes inconsistent with his children – and loses patience with them. He may lose their respect. They may respond by rebelling or may retreat into their shells. He is less sensitive to his

wife's needs and wishes. He is not much company in the evenings if he has been drinking and is now often asleep in a chair. If she complains, he becomes defensive. Temper is less controlled and angry outbursts may become common.

CASE HISTORY: SIMON

Simon had worked hard, step by step, up the Civil Service ladder. As new work practices were introduced, he found himself more and more often drinking after work and collapsing as soon as he arrived home. His wife resented making a meal that he sometimes never touched.

When he stirred himself in time for the 9 p.m. news, he barked at the children. They had been used to a father who was always ready to help with homework or fit for a game of football before supper. His wife told him what was happening, but he seemed to ignore it. She begged him to get some help but he said that she was exaggerating and blamed his bosses. He was stunned and very distressed, when he returned from 2-day meeting in London, to find that she had left with the two children. She had gone to live in a flat that she had rented, leaving only her sister's address through which all messages would henceforth be communicated.

If a mother is drinking too much, the same can happen. She does not cope so well with family responsibilities and so her husband may take control. That may make her angry. The children get used to not taking notice of what she says because when she has been drinking she exaggerates or does not make much sense.

CASE HISTORY: MARY

'Get out of here and find yourself somewhere to live – somewhere selfish people like you can learn the hard way,' Mary screamed. Tina slammed the door, a bit harder than the last time they argued. Her sports bag was already packed together with her railcard and the phone number of her friend from year 11 at school. She knew that her mother could be like this if she'd been drinking all evening, but nowadays it was happening most days. Next morning, Mary would wake in a panic, remembering in a haze her row with her daughter, feeling sick with guilt. Why could she not talk to her any longer, why was it rows always, why was a responsible mother losing hold of her life?

It took Mary another two years to win back Tina's affection and respect, and in that time Mary had to face something that she had hedged around for at least two years before that – a bad-tempered,

hurt and critical side of her came out whenever she drank and she seemed no longer able to control her drinking.

Alcohol can be a significant drain on family finances. Resentments will grow if what used to be spent on a family outing or holiday is now going on drink. Alcohol causes a shrunken bank account more often than it causes a shrunken brain, but both have serious results.

Drinking is one cause of marriages splitting up. Some partners give ample warning of their intention to leave and the drinker may hear and take action. At other times the message is not heard or does not get through. Sometimes a spouse leaves knowing that the relationship has changed but is not clear enough about the cause to make a specific complaint.

When mother or father is drinking in a way that affects the family, it may cause embarrassment. Friends are no longer invited to the house. The drinking problem is kept a secret, as if it was a slur on the family.

Alcohol problems run in families
We explain why this happens on pages 9–10. If mother, father or another close relative has a drink problem, then the next generation should be advised to take great care in using alcohol.

DRINKING TO COPE WITH STRESS

You've all heard someone say, 'Drinking helps me cope' or 'Alcohol is a solution to my problems, not a problem itself' or 'I need a drink to wind down'. Alcohol is a sedative, and if your mind or body is tense alcohol will combat that. If the dose is big enough, alcohol induces sleep.

Research shows, however, that regular drinking to relieve tension can do the opposite. If your nervous system gets used to alcohol, it is as if your nerve cells call out for the next dose. For example, if we regularly take a night-cap to get to sleep, we may find we have difficulty getting off to sleep without one.

CASE HISTORY: ANDREW

Andrew is a salesman who gets tense at work, because of difficult customers and the targets his boss sets him. If he takes a drink at lunch time to relax, he may feel like more on the way home after work. If he next takes a drink in the evening at home, there is some alcohol in the body almost round the clock. Then he will begin to feel more tense and anxious than usual first thing in the morning. He may believe this is due to the worrying thoughts he has about how to face the day, but it may actually be due to the body chemistry 'wanting' the next drink.

Drinking to cope with stress can be counterproductive in another way – it can be tricky to get the amount just right so that anxiety is relieved but performance is still OK. The bride's father who dreads having to make a speech at the reception is occasionally over the top! There are other ways to deal with tension. Here are some tips which have helped many busy people.

Handling tension

● **Set limits on what people demand of you**: we all have a right to say 'No'. It is perfectly reasonable to tell people that you have to put a stop on what, and how much, you take on.

● **Be easier on yourself – and others**: don't aim for perfection. You can do your best, given the circumstances. It is OK to be 'good enough'.

CASE HISTORY: JOHN

John was a perfectionist and proud. He gave himself and his family hell whenever there was some DIY repair job in the house and he failed to get a screw to fit to the last millimetre. When tradesmen came he became vitriolic at any delays.

When his family at last got across to him how pointless his anger was, he began to take a new attitude. He actually started to enjoy taking time to do things, instead of rushing. His

JOHN WAS A PERFECTIONIST...

DAMN-IT
*@♪※+!

HIS VITRIOLIC ANGER WAS TELLING ON HIS FAMILY ...

DAD THIS IS SILLY!

JOHN, CALM DOWN THIS ANGER IS GETTING YOU NOWHERE!

I'M KEEPING THINGS IN PERSPECTIVE.

AT LAST HE'S FINALLY CONTROLLING HIS STRESS.

catch phrase became 'I'm keeping things in perspective'. He learned to live in the present moment, and to take pleasure in that, without continually letting himself feel under pressure.

● **Accept what cannot be changed**: Fight the battles that you can win, not those you cannot win. What is the point of burning up with anger about things that won't change?

● **Delegate!** If you cannot face the household chores after a day at work, get the family to do more. But ask them firmly and clearly, otherwise they may not know you mean it. And make it clear it is to be done properly. In the workplace, people may believe they are delegating, but check whether there is something else others could be doing to relieve you.

● **Check how you react to criticism**: If it was correct, can you learn from it? If the criticism is not correct, remember that others have a right to their opinions. You can agree to disagree.

● **Too much to get done?** If you feel that you have too much to get through, and you start to think 'I can't handle this', then tension builds up. Combat this by pacing yourself and taking on one job at a time.

TIPS TO HELP YOU SLEEP WITHOUT USING ALCOHOL

- Take more physical exercise
- Avoid tea, coffee and other caffeine-containing drinks such as Cola after 6 p.m.
- Go to bed later, having found something interesting and enjoyable to do in the evening – such as read a book or newspaper, do a jigsaw or crossword puzzle or watch a video
- Have a bedtime snack – a small amount of carbohydrate and fat, such as toast and a hot milky drink, has been shown to help sleep
- Relax in a warm bath
- When you go to bed, lie still – you can rest your body without sleeping; a relaxation method can help – such as long slow breaths and letting your muscles flop loose
- Use a self-hypnosis relaxation tape
- If worries fill your head as soon as it touches the pillow, keep a piece of paper handy and write your worries down as they occur. You can tackle them in the morning when your mind is fresh – a tired mind can trick you into thinking a problem is insoluble

DRINKING TO HELP YOU SLEEP

Alcohol is a sedative. A drink at bedtime can help people get off to sleep sooner than they might otherwise. But, as alcohol is burnt up by the body, its level in the blood falls – so if sleep was artificially induced by alcohol there can be a rebound effect causing unpleasant wakefulness at 2 or 3 a.m.

The other disadvantage of alcohol as a sleeping potion is that, if you use it regularly over two or three weeks, your brain's sleep centre expects it and will not switch over into sleep easily without it.

Some people worry when they feel they are not getting enough sleep. They believe in a magic seven or eight hours. But the need for sleep varies greatly and many people need only four or five hours. If they have little to keep them occupied and interested, however, they may start to worry, go to bed earlier and try to sleep more. This can be difficult as sleep cannot be willed – the brain's sleep centre has its own rhythm. Worrying about not getting to sleep is a sure way to stay awake.

If you use sleeping tablets, take care with alcohol because it adds to their effect.

DRINKING TO AVOID 'THE BLUES'

The first effect of alcohol – when the setting and atmosphere are right – is a feeling of well-being. But when the alcohol level in your blood falls back you tend to feel tired and out of sorts. This can lead some people to experience depressed, hopeless feelings and thoughts.

CASE HISTORY: GRANNY SHAW

It was her grandchildren who first said it directly to her. 'Nanny,' as they then called her, 'Why do you always drink sherry?' The loneliness that she had felt since her husband's long incapacity and eventual death was worse because, during those years, she had let her own interests flag and did not keep up with friends. Yet since he died, although she was now free of the burden of his suffering, her life had got even darker. At first, sherry helped, but now it was a habit which she could not, and did not want to, break. It saddened her daughter who had begun to look for a child-minder for

GRANNY SHAW OFTEN LOOKED AFTER HER GRANDCHILDREN...

BUT HER SHERRY DRINKING HAD BECOME A PROBLEM...

WHY DO YOU ALWAYS DRINK SHERRY? GRANNY?

I CAN'T TRUST MUM ANY MORE. I'LL HAVE TO FIND A CHILD-MINDER WHEN I GO BACK TO WORK!

WHY DO I NEVER SEE THEM ANY MORE?

TIPS ON GETTING THROUGH THE WORK

- List jobs by priority. Do the first one and clear it before starting the next
- Pace yourself: we can only get through so much
- Limit interruptions
- Check reality: 'In the past I got through a lot of work, so I'll manage this time as well'
- Papers piling up? If urgent do it; if no action needed, bin it

after school. She was no longer confident that she could safely leave her children with her mother because she was now so erratic. However, that would remove her mother's only contact with other people and she could not bring herself to do so.

If you associate feeling well and happy with the first drink, you may use alcohol to meet a period of depression. Some people are more prone to this than others, and there is an illness in which low mood and pessimism can occur out of the blue, called depressive illness. Meeting good friends and keeping an active social life can be good for depression – but taking a drink as a remedy is usually not good medicine.

The way to recover is to get our thinking straight, improve our relationships with others and have a variety of interests and activities. Here are some points which people have found more helpful than drinking alcohol when they find that depression, or 'nervous exhaustion' as it is sometimes called, threatens to take them over.

- **Depression is a form of fatigue:** It is as if your mental batteries are low and you need to recharge them. While the batteries are low, your brain may not be as efficient as usual, so be easy on yourself. It passes. It may lift as suddenly as it came. Or you get better in steps, with some bad days but more and more good days.

- **Challenge faulty thinking**: For example, one person may criticise something you did – that does not mean you are 'totally incapable' if the reality is that most of the time you do things correctly.

- **Keep your perspective:** If something has gone wrong take care you are not making a catastrophe out of it. You may have made an error, but that does not write you off totally. You still are the person you are, with your qualities and weaker spots, your experience and your skills. It cannot logically be the end of the world.

- **Avoid mind-reading**: Do not immediately jump to a negative conclusion. Do you sometimes think, automatically, that people are thinking the worst of you? If so, you may react defensively or even aggressively to someone before they say or do anything. Friendships or enjoyable occasions can be spoiled this way. Don't try to read minds. We cannot tell what others are thinking or feeling until they tell us. It does not always matter what others are thinking – do what makes you feel better.

- **Avoid living by fixed rules**: If you have excessively high expectations you set yourself up for feeling like a failure. Thinking 'I must' or 'I should' can lead to guilt or disappointment if you do not achieve all your targets. Be easier on yourself (and others!). Be more forgiving. Say 'I should like to' or 'I prefer to' instead of the tyrannical 'musts' and 'shoulds'.

- **Keep an open mind**: If you bring in history ('here we go again' or 'it's always like this for me') you

IT'S OBVIOUS THEY DON'T LIKE ME!

stop letting it get under your skin. Why give them the satisfaction of seeing you go under?

● **Speak up for yourself:** This helps you value yourself more – and you'll find that others will too. Be open and direct, using 'I would like', 'I feel' or 'No, I do not wish to'. Speak calmly and concisely, but firmly. Repeat what you have to say if necessary, to be sure you have been heard. Don't use alcohol for this – people may think it's the drink talking or you may come across as aggressive. Do not insist on winning every point, just the

stop yourself having new experiences and miss out on openings and chances.

● **Avoid black and white thinking**: No-one, including you, is totally successful or a total loser. If you hear yourself thinking any of the 'totallys', take care. Do not write someone off because he or she made a mistake. That includes you.

● **Look out for the 'poor-me's'**: If you find yourself thinking 'no-one knows what I'm going through', this could be wasting valuable emotional energy. It may frighten off those who would like to help you. Sometimes it can help to remind yourself that there are people worse off. If you really have had a bad deal, try to work out how you can

ones that are important to you. Being aggressive may alienate others. When you feel angry about something someone has done, you can say, 'When you do that I feel angry. This is what I would prefer you to do instead'. In this way they may see something they did not see before. Others will only know what you want and feel, if you put it into words. Do not rely on telepathy!

● **Deal with loneliness**: We need contact with others. The loss of a loved one or the break-up of a relationship can leave you feeling numbed. But it is vital to start meeting old friends and making new ones as soon as possible. Do not be discouraged if your first attempts come to nothing. Clubs, churches, offering your services to a voluntary organisation, attending classes are all possible. Check your local newspaper or the public library notice board.

● **Boredom is a serious medical condition!** There must be something out there in a world of such diversity to interest you. Learn poetry, become a bonsai expert, take a car maintenance course – anything!

Finally, your doctor can prescribe medication for depressive illness which helps gradually over a period of three to six weeks. It is important to persevere through any initial side effects you may feel. Alcohol may interfere with the effect of antidepressants. If you want to have a drink, and that does not go against your doctors' instructions or any goal that you have set yourself to abstain, then take a maximum of only one drink (i.e. half a pint of beer or one glass of wine) if taking antidepressants, and never mix that with driving (see page 67).

KEY POINTS

✓ A family may try to hide the fact that someone is drinking too much

✓ Alcohol can make sleep disturbed

✓ Alcohol can make depression worse

✓ There are mental techniques for getting out of tension and depression

How to recognise a drinking problem

If the unwanted effects of drinking are harming your life in some way – your health, your relationships with those you care about, your work – then you have a drinking problem. If you are beginning to need alcohol and find it hard to take it or leave it, or it is becoming difficult to control the amount you drink, then you are becoming 'dependent' on alcohol and that can cause other problems to develop. Ask yourself the following questions and be frank about the answers.

Are there changes in relationships?

The pleasant releasing effect of drinking allows you to 'let your hair down' – which can also alienate people and hurtful things may be said. After drinking, as the level of alcohol in your blood falls, you can get bad-tempered and irritable. Drinkers can get touchy – seeing slights where none was intended. Bottled up envy or jealousy may come out in a destructive way. If large quantities of alcohol are drunk, the memory can be patchy for some of these moments – moments that may have been very upsetting for others.

Commitments may be skipped, or even forgotten: a father lets his son down over a promised outing to a football match; a mother loses interest in her teenage daughter's fashion pursuits.

There may be repercussions throughout the family – children become defiant, sulky or unhappy. They do less well at school. The spouse grows cold or distant, hurt by things said, and by the arguments which develop about the drinking.

Friendships are sometimes damaged in a similar way. People who drink a lot may also develop a habit of phoning friends when intoxicated, perhaps at unsociable hours, and pouring out their troubles in an insensitive way.

Are there changes in my work performance?
Frequent lateness at work or sick

leave can signal that an employee is drinking too much, resulting in hangovers the next day. Employers may overlook odd days off, but colleagues who have to bear the brunt of absences may be less patient. Drinkers often think that no-one notices extended lunch breaks (to get a drink) or the smell of alcohol on their breath.

Have I become dependent?

Has life become more oriented around places, occasions and company where there is going to be a drink? Previous hobbies or interests may get displaced in favour of drinking. Instead of just wanting a drink the feeling is of actually needing a drink. This is due to a mixture of habit and a chemical process, to which some people may be more prone than others.

When people with this pattern of drinking try to cut down, they may find it very difficult. The thought of a drink is strongly triggered in situations where they used to drink or when they are with the same friends.

How dependent have I become?

In the early stages, our brain cells become used to alcohol, so that a rebound of sudden tension or anxiety occurs if brain cells are deprived of alcohol, when the next drink is not there. This feeling may

EARLY SIGNS OF DEPENDENCE

- Drinking pattern tending to be the same each day
- Setting a limit but not sticking to it
- Giving up activities which do not involve drink
- Having some problems caused by drinking but not noticing, and/or letting it happen again
- A larger amount needed to give the same effect

LATER SIGNS OF DEPENDENCE

- Sleep problems
- Nervous, sickly, sweaty or shaky in the morning
- Regularly having a drink within 3 hours of waking
- Sometimes severe withdrawal symptoms: these are epileptic seizures, when people suddenly go unconscious hours or days after stopping drinking, perhaps with jerking of the arms and legs and interrupted breathing; and delirium tremens, when people become confused, not knowing where they are or who they are with, and can have hallucinations

be mistaken for anxiety about going to work, worry about the family, or some other connection the person has made. Drinkers may not readily see, or wish to see, the connection between these feelings and the fact that they have got into a very regular pattern of drinking in recent weeks or months.

Another sign of early dependence in drinkers is when they drink much more than they intend. They may say they feel they cannot control their drinking as well as they used to – although they may have had poor control from early in their drinking days.

Friends and family may recognise the trouble, but remain helpless because people who are developing a drink problem often see things differently, as they have become attached to drinking and do not want to admit it is time to cut back.

When the problem goes to the next stage, the rebound feelings may be accompanied by tremor of the hands or fingers, especially in the morning when the blood alcohol level is low. A feeling of butterflies in the stomach may be there too, or nausea when the teeth are brushed or breakfast contemplated. A drink settles this – and so drinking in the morning becomes a habit.

The rebound symptoms are also called withdrawal symptoms. If someone has been drinking 16 or more units per day, for several weeks, and then stops for some reason, these can be very unpleasant. At their severest, an epileptic fit can occur, or a temporary delirious state when the person loses touch with reality and has hallucinations (delirium tremens or 'DTs'). It is very important to avoid such a severe reaction and medication from a doctor can prevent it, if taken at the point drinking stops.

A mysterious feature of dependence on alcohol is the ease with which the cycle of abstinence, drinking and dependence can be repeated. If a person stops drinking for some days, weeks or even months and then takes another drink, the vicious circle starts all over again. They have a period of wanting to drink, then drinking, followed by stopping and withdrawal symptoms returning. After another few days or weeks, the cycle starts over again.

Is dependence an illness?

People dependent on alcohol drink in response to triggers – for example avoiding withdrawal symptoms, or in certain emotional states. The memories of pleasurable feelings from alcohol have been laid down deep in the brain. This pattern of drinking

from habit has been seen in animals studied in scientific laboratories. Some families of animals pass on a genetic tendency to alcohol dependence – so there is strong evidence for biological factors.

Someone who is dependent on alcohol has tremendous struggles about whether or not to drink, which most of us never know. But, although there may be a biological basis to this, his or her recovery will depend on how hard an effort is made, as well as how much help is received.

KEY POINTS

✓ Dependence on alcohol means beginning to 'need' it on some occasions, or repeatedly failing to control the amount

✓ Some dependent drinkers get withdrawal symptoms when they cut down or go without

✓ There is a chemical basis to dependence on alcohol, but change means wanting to change and making an effort

How to change your drinking pattern

DO I NEED TO CUT DOWN?

If you are wondering whether you should change your drinking pattern, weigh up the benefits of drinking against the costs. You can make a list of the pros and cons of your drinking – try to be objective when you do this. Think about changing your drinking pattern if the disadvantages of drinking outweigh the advantages.

Solution or cause

Is drinking the solution to your problems or the cause? Drinking eats up money and brain cells forever but has never made problems disappear for more than an hour or

PROS AND CONS OF DRINKING: EXAMPLE

ADVANTAGES	DISADVANTAGES
• Enjoy the pub atmosphere	• Cost
• Helps me relax	• Drink is affecting my job
• Feel I talk better after one or two	• My family get upset by it
• Makes me feel less shy with the opposite sex	• Sex life isn't so good
	• Gives me sickness and stomach pain

two. If you have been using alcohol for tension, you might have begun to think of it as a friend rather than a foe. However, please read pages 33–5 about alcohol and stress, because alcohol can make tension and depression worse.

For some, the problem is criticism about drinking by their spouse or employer, not the drinking itself. But you may have been wearing blinkers – alcohol can definitely blur your memory. Perhaps you have been playing down or not even registering things you did or said after drinking.

You may be someone who can drink with enjoyment and without any problems usually, but find that just sometimes your drinking goes way over what is safe or right for the occasion. Some people find it very difficult, or impossible, to predict whether, when they have a drink, it will end up with trouble.

Am I at risk?

You may find that the disadvantages do not at present outweigh the advantages but you want to know if you are at risk. Over 28 units per week for men (14 for women) means that you may begin to run into problems.

Remember alcoholism runs in families. Take care if your grandparents, uncles, aunts or members of your immediate family have had a drinking problem – you may have inherited some genes which make you more vulnerable (see pages 9–10).

TAKE ACTION!
Cutting down

If your drinking has begun to cause problems, you will have to make a radical change if you want to be able to carry on drinking but do it safely. It will mean reducing the days on which you drink, making the maximum amount on any occasion very small, such as 3 units, so that you do not start dissolving your good intentions with alcohol. It will probably

mean changing the situations where you drink – setting a rule never to drink alone, avoiding certain heavy drinking friends and settings.

Stopping

You may know that the best way for you is to keep it simple – to quit. Or maybe you have tried cutting down but failed. Here are some tips on how to succeed.

● **Remember why**: Always keep fresh in your mind why you have decided to quit.

● **The first few days are the worst**: Sweating, tremor, anxiety,

STOP DRINKING COMPLETELY IF ANY OF THESE APPLY

- Symptoms of dependence (see page 45) for more than a month
- Your partner is not in full agreement with your plan for limited drinking
- You are easily upset or do things on the spur of the moment
- You are not good at sticking to rules – stopping is simpler to do and simpler for family and friends to understand
- One of your body's organs is damaged
- You have an emotional illness

TIPS TO CUT DOWN DRINKING

- List your reasons for cutting down
- Set rules (realistic ones), e.g. 'Saturdays only'; 'never alone'; 'no more than four units a day'
- Enlist help from family and friends
- Change to a lower strength drink
- Practise saying 'No'
- Sip, don't gulp – pace your drinking
- Avoid heavy drinking friends and buying rounds
- Eat something when drinking
- Don't drink if depressed or angry
- Setback? Figure out why you slipped and how to avoid repeating it. Try again
- If it's not working, try a month or two of not drinking at all to see if that's more successful

'butterflies in the stomach', not sleeping, nausea and perhaps vomiting, can occur in the first two or three days after stopping drinking. You could avoid this by cutting down gradually over seven days, but some people find that hard and prefer to set a date and stop. The urge to take alcohol may be strong.

- **Coping with withdrawal symptoms**: Only very unpleasant in someone who was drinking 15 or more units per day (half a bottle of spirits, 5 to 6 pints of beer). Tranquillisers prescribed by a doctor could be helpful, assuming you are going to stop all alcohol. Drinking 30 units per day (a bottle of spirits or 12 pints of beer) could mean serious withdrawal symptoms such as epileptic fits and you must get medical help to reduce the effects of withdrawal.

Tranquillisers are usually only taken for four or five days and at most for 10 days. You start with the largest dose in the first 24 hours after your last drink and tail them off until you are taking one tablet or capsule at night on the last night. **Do not take alcohol once you have started the course of tranquillisers.**

- **Sleeping**: Sleep may be disturbed, but that never harmed anyone. Ways to relax could include taking time off work, having a warm bath at night, listening to favourite music, going for walks, or keeping occupied. The sleep pattern gradually returns to normal after about one or two weeks.

- **Take regular meals**: Eat regularly and drink fruit juice or milk. Avoid lots of tea and coffee because caffeine will increase the anxiety of the withdrawal period, prevent sleep and could increase the urge to drink. Getting hungry can also lead to wanting a drink.

- **Come clean**: It is probably best to tell close friends and relatives that you have stopped drinking and admit it had been becoming a problem. If you make up a reason such as 'I'm on tablets from the doctor', then in a week or two they will once more be putting pressure on you to take a drink.

- **Practise refusing**: Practise saying 'No' convincingly, so that you are ready when people offer you a drink.

- **Keep at it**: Complacency is the main reason why people relapse. You will find that after you have stayed off alcohol for a few weeks, you feel confident that you can now handle it. This may not be true. You may find that quite quickly, even over a few days, your old drinking pattern re-emerges.

- **Take up a hobby**: If drinking took up your time, or was your main hobby, you will need to find a substitute activity. Take up a new interest or one you dropped some years ago. Getting physically fit is a hobby with extra pay-offs!

- **First drink**: Staying away from that first drink is the key to success.

GETTING EXTRA HELP
Medical treatment

- **Discussion and advice**: Your doctor's main role will be to answer questions you have about drinking and your health, to help you work out the pros and cons of your drinking and, if you decide to make a change, to help you make a plan of action.

- **Medication for withdrawal symptoms**: If you have decided to stop drinking, your doctor can assess whether you need a prescription to control withdrawal symptoms. He or she may suggest a tranquilliser, probably diazepam or chlordiazepoxide. The largest dose is for the first 24 hours after the last drink, followed by a step-wise reduction over the next three to five days. Tranquillisers should not be continued for longer than two weeks, because dependence develops and another vicious circle can be started, where the person feels a strong need for the tablets and gets anxious without them.

- **Vitamins**: Your doctor may prescribe vitamin tablets for you – or you can buy them from your pharmacist. Vitamin B_1, thiamine, is the most important for a drinker. In hospital, the vitamins may be given by injection into a vein or muscle, because alcohol can damage the body's ability to absorb vitamins taken by mouth.

- **Deterrent tablets**: Some substances react with alcohol to give a very unpleasant reaction. For example, if you eat the mushroom, inky nightcap, and then drink alcohol, your face goes red and your head and heart pound. Disulfiram (Antabuse) is a medication that acts in the same way.

If you have been taking one of these regularly, in a sufficient dose, and then take even small amounts of alcohol, within about 15 minutes your face feels hot and burning, your head and heart pound, your breathing feels tight and you may vomit or faint. It is a very unpleasant feeling and for someone with heart disease or on powerful drugs for lowering blood pressure, it could even be fatal.

Disulfiram has a long action, once a sufficient starting dose has been taken. An alcohol reaction can occur up to seven days later. The tablets (seven per week) can be taken once a day or spaced out with three one day and two on two other days. As with many medications, some people may notice side effects and have to decide whether or not to continue.

You could arrange with someone to remind you to take it. Otherwise you may 'forget' to take your tablets if you still partly want to drink. You can give confidence to your partner or your employer by letting them see you take your tablet – in which case you should dissolve it in water so that you are not tempted to put it under your tongue and spit it out later! This is called the 'partnership approach'.

Using deterrent tablets is not a sign of weakness. It is a strength to recognise that will-power is not always there when you need it most. The choice to drink or not to drink is still yours – and you make it each time you take a tablet. If you find this method works for you, keep it up for 6 to 12 months. This gives time to see that life without alcohol is possible and weakens some of your old habits and triggers to drinking.

● **Help for anxiety and fears**: Some anxious people find they gradually become calmer after they stop drinking and do not need further help. If anxiety or panicky feelings continue, finding ways to relax and control anxiety or overcome fears by facing the feared situation (called exposure therapy) can be all that is needed.

Tranquillisers such as diazepam are best avoided because you can become dependent on them. Drugs used for depression can help anxiety, panic attacks and some phobias. These are not addictive and can be safely used for months or even years.

● **Treatment for depressive illness**: You may need this if you experience a low, hopeless or worried feeling, which goes on for weeks and cannot be linked to anything particular going wrong. This is not the low or fed up feeling we have when we have had a bad day – unless we plan to wallow in it, we are probably OK by next morning. In depressive illness, the sufferer loses the ability to experience fun and joy, is caught up in pessimistic thoughts, is irritable, easily tired and may feel undue guilt. They may even feel so worthless and hopeless that they have thoughts of suicide. They tend to wake in the small hours and lie awake worrying. Their appetite may decrease and they may lose interest in sex. Alcohol is a very bad treatment for depression. Avoid it completely, or at most have one drink (half a pint of beer or one glass of wine) only very occasionally, and do not mix with driving.

There is a good chance of full recovery from depressive illness. Psychotherapy – talking therapy –

with a counsellor, doctor or psychologist will help you keep your thoughts in perspective and prevent them spiralling downwards. The therapy will help you regain a belief in your own qualities and not let comments by others or feelings of resentment fester and cause inner anger.

The chemical changes in your brain which go with depression can be corrected by getting your thoughts in order and getting more enjoyment from relationships and your life. In addition, antidepressants can help to correct these changes. They can be used for several months – or even for years by people who tend to have relapses of the illness and therefore need a preventive strategy. Side effects vary depending on the type of tablet prescribed, and are only common in the first three to four days.

Some types have a sedative effect which can immediately help sleep but could interfere with driving. Other types can cause nausea or anxiety in the first few days, although this usually passes. Antidepressants take three to six weeks to have their main effect, so it is important to give them a fair chance to work.

Specialist centres
There are National Health Service and private clinics offering treatment for alcohol dependence. Private clinics tend to be residential and may be costly, whereas in the Health Service you are usually seen and treated as an outpatient. In Britain it is usual to make contact with specialist clinics through your GP but you do not have to do this if you strongly prefer to refer yourself direct, perhaps because you fear (possibly quite unreasonably) your GP's reaction.

The clinics use group therapy to overcome shame and secrecy – you meet others with whom you can identify. It helps you to see things in a broader perspective, as well as to get tips on how to handle life without alcohol. People gain in strength and confidence with group therapy. This can help with the social anxiety that some drinkers have struggled with – boosting self-confidence and teaching how to be constructively assertive.

The clinic will probably want to have contact with your family too. It is important to have your family's views on what has been happening and what help is needed and the clinic may have useful advice for them.

Counselling
Many cities have 'alcohol advice centres' or 'Councils on Alcohol' giving individual guidance and support. The counsellors are trained, lay volunteers. These centres are listed in your local telephone directory.

Alcoholics Anonymous

AA is a fellowship of men and women who have an honest desire to stop drinking. They have recognised that they are 'powerless over alcohol'. Experience has shown them that by meeting together and living by simple, sensible guidelines – such as 'take life one day at a time' – they can stay away from the first drink. The atmosphere is warm and welcoming.

Some repetitiveness at the meetings is deliberate. People who have had a drink problem know how easy it is to forget the problems alcohol caused. When they forget, the next relapse is one step nearer. At AA people keep the memory of those problems fresh in their minds, resisting the temptation we all have to gloss over past pain.

There is a 'spiritual' element to AA. Although you may hear people talking about God or a Higher Power at AA, there are many atheists who have found AA has helped them enormously. There are AA groups in most countries of the world and it is not linked to any church or religion.

Meeting members of AA can give hope to you if you are still in the midst of your problem and fear it is insuperable. There are some

people who will never overcome their drink problem unless they draw regularly on the strength and companionship to be found at AA.

The contact for your local AA group is listed in your local telephone directory.

Recent discoveries

Painstaking research into chemical disturbance in the brain underlying the dependence on alcohol has led to two new drugs: acamprosate and naltrexone. They work differently but both reduce the craving for alcohol which often continues for some months in alcohol-dependent individuals when they stop drinking. They have been effective in increasing abstinence and reducing the frequency of relapse and the amount of drinking. Both are safe and usually do not cause side effects, and neither is addictive. They are not a form of tranquilliser, which could be abused or lead to another addiction.

If a person should happen to drink alcohol while on one or other of these drugs, there is no unpleasant or dangerous reaction. Nor does it increase the dampening effect that alcohol has on driving or other skills.

They are effective only if taken regularly (acamprosate three times per day and naltrexone once daily), and have been assessed only when counselling or other therapy for

alcohol is undertaken. Some people benefit greatly from one or other of these drugs whereas others do not. The reason for the difference is not yet known. Doctors are only just learning how best these exciting new developments should be incorporated into their therapy package.

KEY POINTS

✓ Some who develop alcohol problems can't successfully cut down. If that's not working, get help to quit completely

✓ Try Alcoholics Anonymous – it's a very successful method

✓ If you're determined but still cannot stick to it, consider deterrent tablets or the new anti-craving medicines

✓ Keep the whole family in the picture

Advice for family, friends and colleagues

DON'T COVER UP

Family and friends, colleagues and supervisors typically try to shield someone with a drink problem, at least initially. They make excuses and cover up, believing that the drinker will soon realise what is happening and do something to put it right. The drinking may, however, become more fixed as dependence intensifies. Praying for a miracle to happen is not usually the answer. Sympathy on its own may achieve nothing – or even enable more drinking. Unless drinkers face the consequences of how alcohol affects them, they just go on repeating the same mistakes.

It can be helpful and constructive to say something to get the drinker to take stock, but sensitivity is necessary. Remember that the drinker has many positive qualities and that the subject of complaint is only the drinking and the behaviour it brings. There is no need to write off the whole person.

Control may be counterproductive

If someone is determined to drink, there is little anyone can do until there is a change of mind. To try and control the situation can be exhausting and frustrating – although you may want to intervene if there is danger of awful consequences – for example,

drinking and driving. However, if you let go of your efforts to control, you not only save your energy – you can also remove one of the drinker's excuses for drinking. He or she cannot blame you for the drinking because you are nagging or bossy. But don't stop giving a firm message that you insist on some change.

Getting things out in the open

Drinkers may fool themselves about the quantity they drink and its harmful consequences. This is partly because they cannot always remember what they did when they drank a lot. It is also because if they admit there is a problem then it would be logical to give up

some drinking. If they still enjoy it or feel they need it, that would be a painful conclusion to reach. This is what is meant by denial.

The more head-on the confrontation, the more denial there can be. It is better to start a discussion with open-ended questions such as 'How are you feeling these days?', 'What are your concerns at present?', leading to 'How do you think your drinking might fit into the picture?'

Choose your timing. Do not expect to be able to talk usefully if tempers are raised or the brain clouded by drink. The 'morning after' may be a good time – or when there has been a crisis.

Let the drinker know what you can and cannot tolerate. Be ready to admit where you have gone wrong and accept criticism if it is justified – but do not take any blame for the drinking. That is entirely the responsibility of the drinker.

Idle threats, or threats you cannot follow through, are pointless. At work, sanctions should be put in writing. At home, make it clear what your needs are and be prepared to negotiate – not about the drinking, but about other ways in which life could be improved by changes on both sides.

If there's no change

In a family, this means that life has to go on and you and your children have to survive. There are different ways in which you can get outside help (see pages 53–9). Keeping the emotional temperature down may help prevent the family from doing things they would later regret. Sometimes couples separate if a drinker cannot or will not take steps to cut back.

Help for the family

Counselling agencies often provide support and advice for partners as well as the drinker and there are self-help groups.

Al-Anon is a wonderful self-help fellowship for families and friends of those with drinking problems and Al-Ateen is for teenage sons and daughters. The contacts of local groups can be found in your local telephone directory.

Living with someone with a drink problem can be taxing and depressing. Al-Anon helps you keep yourself strong and well, and stops you getting eaten up with guilt, anger or frustration. The message is 'detach with love' rather than exhaust yourself struggling with someone else's addiction.

There is a limit to what we can do if our partner, friend or relative wants to drink and is dependent on alcohol. You will get no advice on how to track down the hidden alcohol supplies or catch out the secret drinker in his or her lair – but you may find yourself feeling calmer and less consumed with tension and resentments!

KEY POINTS

✓ A drink problem doesn't mean writing off the whole person

✓ The family should give a clear message

✓ The drinker is the only one responsible for the drinking, but others should accept criticism if it is justified

Children, teenagers and parents

CHILDREN, ALCOHOL AND THE LAW

Under the Licensing Act of 1902, it is an offence to be drunk in charge of a child under the age of seven on any highway, public house, licensed premises, public place, building or inn.

The Children's Act of 1908 banned the use of alcohol on any child under the age of five except for medicinal purposes, and banned children under the age of 14 from the bar of a licensed premise. The Licensing Act of 1964 stated that no one under the age of 18 can be employed in a bar.

At 14 a child can be taken into a bar, but must not consume alcohol. At 16 he or she can buy and drink wine, beer or cider in a restaurant. No

intoxicating liquor can be sold or delivered to a person under 18 years of age.

It has been suggested that for newly qualified drivers age 18 to 20 – the age when road accidents are most common – the legal limit for drinking and driving should be lower than 80 mg% or even zero. However, it is good to see that many young people nowadays have a rule about not drinking any alcohol if they are driving.

CLUBS, PUBS, PARTIES AND TEENAGERS

Going out for a drink is as much part of life for teenagers as it is for adults – perhaps even more, because being with your friends seems to be essen-

tial at that age. The popular meeting places often depend on the profits from serving alcohol, including student unions at college and university.

Some young people overdo it from early on in their drinking days. Some will run into difficulties by drinking and driving, having an accident or falling out with friends. Some will start drinking to solve a problem – a habit which over the coming months or years could lead to major problems. That applies if it is drinking to help shyness or drinking because of being fed-up or bored.

Advice to young people

Let your friends, parents or a school counsellor help if you have worries.

There may be another way round the problem. You may just need to be told that being the quiet, shy person in your group of friends is OK – no-one wants you to be incredibly talkative or witty anyhow!

Saying 'No' can be hard if you are already self-conscious about how you fit in with your group. However, keeping your head and not giving way to pressure shows you have personality. You have the right to say 'No'.

Advice to parents

- Introduce sensible drinking at home if your teenagers say they would like a drink.

- Advise eating something, even some crisps or chips, if they are out drinking with their friends, to help them avoid getting drunk.
- No drinking when driving, cycling or swimming.
- Let them know what the law is on drinking – for example, the minimum age for buying alcohol in a bar, off-licence or supermarket is 18.
- Is your own drinking pattern setting an example you would like them to copy? Our children tend to follow what they see us do more than what we tell them to do!

KEY POINTS

✓ Young people with worries should get help by talking to someone

✓ Children tend to follow what their parents do, not what they say

Drinking, driving, working and the law

DRINKING AND DRIVING

One-quarter of all road traffic fatalities have blood alcohol levels over the legal limit. This increases to 60 per cent for deaths occurring between 10 p.m. and 4 a.m. The greatest number of such fatalities are in the 20–24 year age group. Random roadside tests by the Department of Transport reveal that 17 per cent of people driving between 10 p.m. and 3 a.m .are over the limit.

The law in Britain states that you must not drive, or be in charge of a car, if you are unfit to drive, or have more than 80 milligrams of alcohol in 100 millilitres of blood (80 mg%). This is the same as 35 milligrams in 1000 millilitres (1 litre) of breath. This

level of alcohol in your blood is reached after drinking four to five units of alcohol in one or two hours. Or you could have that level in your blood stream several hours after your last drink, or even the next day, if you had drunk a lot. But people vary and drinking the same amount of alcohol will give different levels in different people. A higher level is reached if you are small or if you are drinking on an empty stomach.

It is also an offence to fail to provide a specimen for analysis while attempting to drive. Conviction for driving over the limit means a fine, a ban from driving for at least a year and higher insurance premiums. If your blood alcohol level is two and a half times above the legal limit, or if it is a second offence in 10 years, or if you refuse to give a breath or blood sample, then before your licence is returned after the ban you have to pass a medical examination to check that you do not still have a drinking problem. This is called the 'High Risk Offender Scheme'. Repeated offences may result in a jail term.

Driving is impaired in many people well below the legal limit of 80 mg%. Even after 2 units (one pint of beer or two glasses of wine), giving a blood alcohol level of around 30 mg%, many drivers have slower reactions and make errors at the wheel. Apart from the personal consequences consider the tragedy you can inflict on others.

DRINKING AND WORK

In most work places, it is a breach of discipline to be under the influence of alcohol at work. This would lead to a warning, either verbal or written. If performance was being impaired by the hangover effects of drinking, this could lead to comment. Being frequently absent from work might be another cause for a warning. The manager might also notice a pattern, such as frequent Monday absences or (if pay day is Thursday!) frequent Friday absences. Frequent time off for vague complaints – gastritis, 'flu, 'nervous tension', 'stress' – is also more common in a worker who is developing a drinking problem.

Many employers have a policy for staff who may have a drinking problem. The object is to encourage recovery as soon as possible, while protecting the workplace and other employees from danger. They may not want to dismiss a highly trained colleague who, when sober, is a very good worker.

It is usually easier to recover from a drink problem if you are still in work, so it is good that some managers pick up a problem in an employee at an early stage and take steps before dismissal is necessary. Otherwise managers and colleagues may say nothing, hoping the drinker will see the obvious and do something about it. If the problem goes on, praying for a miracle is less effective than saying something direct to the person. It is better not to keep on covering up, doing the job for him or her, or making excuses. The sooner someone brings the problem into the open the better.

If there has been a disciplinary issue, the employer may require the employee to seek advice or be examined by the occupational health physician of the company. The employee who chooses to follow this route may be expected to seek outside help and agree to the helping agency (counselling service or clinic) giving a report on progress to the employer. The report would not normally give any personal details, but states whether or not the individual is attending appointments and following advice.

KEY POINTS

✓ Even below the legal alcohol limit, driving can still be erratic after drinking

✓ A drink–drive offence means a ban, or a fine and higher insurance

✓ If an employee's drinking affects work, it is better to bring it up than to cover it up

Useful addresses

Alcoholics Anonymous
AA meetings are found world-wide.
Check your local phone directory or
newspaper.

National number at local rates,
giving local information 24 hours a
day: 0345 697555

For literature and world-wide
contacts:
PO Box 1
Stonebow House
Stonebow, York YO1 7NJ
Tel: 01904 644026 (9am – 5pm)

Northern Ireland
Tel: 01232 681 084

**Al-Anon Family Groups (also
Al-Ateen)**
61 Great Dover St
London SE1 4YF
Tel: 0171 403 0888

**Councils on alcohol, alcohol
advice centres, clinics**
Local phone directory.

Alcohol Concern
Waterbridge House
32–36 Loman Street
London SE1 0EE
Tel: 0171 928 7377

or

Scottish Council on Alcohol
Second Floor, 166 Buchanan Street
Glasgow G1 2NH
Tel: 0141 333 9677
Fax: 0141 333 1606

Index